The surrealist poet, Jerry Edwards, lives in the Sonoran Desert of Arizona. His home is literally in the shadows of the Catalina Mountains. He describes himself as a 12-year-old boy, disguised as an 82-year-old grandfather. He's also said that he'd once been a 12-year-old boy, disguised as a business executive.

This anthology of poetry, *Venus – A Point of Expression*, is his second publication of poetry in as many years. His first book, *Memories in Technicolor*, was released in June 2023. A reader, critiquing his writing, commented that he was obviously, "a hopeless romantic". Edwards pleads guilty to the description!

This anthology of verse is dedicated to two women that have been positive forces in my life.

The first dedication is to my mother: Claudia Loraine Edwards. She was a Southern woman of imagination and inspired spiritual beliefs. She believed that all components of the physical world – all life, had a central base of commonality. She was well read, intelligent, devoted to her family and resolute in the pursuit of being the best person that she could be.

Once in a parent-teachers meeting my homeroom teacher, Mrs. Greene, told my mother that I was not properly concentrating in class. She said that I spent an inordinate amount of time day-dreaming, or surreptitiously reading adventure novels.

My mother smiled knowingly and replied that I was just fine; that during those times I was involved in a story inside my imagination. My mother, an only child, once told me that her imagination was her best, most trusted advisor and friend when she was a girl. Some components of her personality are found in the poem, in this book: Loraine.

So, Mom, you gave me the gift of life and the gift of creatively day-dreaming -sometimes when I should have been working!

The second dedication is to my sweetheart, Carole Clendenon Edwards. We spent forty-seven great years together in a never -ending series of adventure. She was my lover, companion, best friend and advisor. She has recently gone through that blue-tunnel of mystery, into another dimension due to the ravages of Parkinson's Disease. I'm certain: that somewhere, somehow, we will reconnect again! The poem, in this volume, 'She Dances in The Trees,' is dedicated to her compelling memory.

Jerry Edwards

VENUS – A POINT OF EXPRESSION

AUSTIN MACAULEY PUBLISHERS™

LONDON * CAMBRIDGE * NEW YORK * SHARJAH

Ordering Information
Quantity sales: Special discounts are available on quantity purchases by corporations, associations, and others. For details, contact the publisher at the address below.

Publisher's Cataloging-in-Publication data
Edwards, Jerry
Venus – A Point of Expression

ISBN 9798891552968 (Paperback)
ISBN 9798891552975 (Hardback)
ISBN 9798891552982 (ePub e-book)

Library of Congress Control Number: 2023921395

www.austinmacauley.com/us

First Published 2024
Austin Macauley Publishers LLC
40 Wall Street, 33rd Floor, Suite 3302
New York, NY 10005
USA

mail-usa@austinmacauley.com
+1 (646) 5125767

I became enamored with surrealistic poetry as a young person. Walt Whitman's *Leaves of Grass* was inspirational to me. All of the poetry by Dylan Thomas became my 'carry around bible.' Although Thomas often denied that he was a surrealist writer… anyone that knew poetry knew better. Later Alan Ginsberg's *Howl* was a treasured delight. I didn't quite understand all of it when I was 15… I hardly understand it any better today!

Later I read Andre Breton, the principal theorist of Surrealism, concluding that it loses something in translation, although no doubt the works of a serious and talented writer. John Ashbery's *Self Portrait in a Convex Mirror* has been resident in my home library since he won the Pulitzer Prize for poetry and National Book Award in 1972. In contemporary poetry, he is the benchmark, that to which any poet would aspire.

I want to acknowledge that reading these gifted poets was where I learned to craft words into verse, with the minimum talent that I have. There are many others also, that I want to thank for my self-taught education… You know who you are.

Table of Contents

Venus in the Sky Is a Point of Expression	13
Sometimes I Wonder Why	14
Alone	15
The Sound of Heaven	16
The Blue Tunnel into Tomorrow	17
Jesse Dances in L.A.	18
I Dream of Flying	19
Why Have You Then	20
The Trees Come Down at Night	21
The Lives of Sacred Trees	22
April Is Her Name	24
The Sound That Colors Make	25
Lost Like Me	27
I Sing as the Ocean	28
She Dances in the Trees	29
It Was in the Summer	30
My Hometown	31
Alvarado Street	32
Let There Be Light	33
Off Biloxi – An Uncertain Day	34

July   35

Return from Nowhere   36

Loraine   38

An Imperfect Expectation   40

What Is a Heart   41

The Sun Can Rise So Quickly   43

I Still Think of You Late at Night   44

The Spring Rain   45

A Rainbow Fell   46

The Light Slowly Moves Across   47

Do You Remember the Summer?   48

The Bruha Katrina   49

No Cold Stone Can Hide Her   51

Lost in America   52

Two Generations in the Repose of Sleep   53

Writing in the Night   54

Morning Rain   55

A Cold Slice of the Moon   56

On the Ridge Road to Summerland   57

Your Laughter Hung in the Air   58

When Tommy Died   59

A Storm Is Coming   60

The Thoughts Behind Your Smile   61

Is Music More Than Black Patches   62

September Is a Brown Warm Song   63

I Often Think of Someone I Knew Long Ago   64

The Rising Sun Brought a Textured Morning   65

He Held a Lotus Flower in His Hands   66

Somewhere a Woman Is Crying   67

Time   68

I Wonder Where   69

Underneath the Whispers   70

The Ruined South   71

One   72

Two   73

Three   74

Four   76

Five   78

Six   79

Seven   80

Eight   81

Nine   82

Ten   83

Eleven   84

Twelve   85

Thirteen   87

Fourteen   89

Fifteen   90

Venus in the Sky Is a Point of Expression

The infinite sky above the earth
is a blue to black expanse of mystery
from day – until night, the lights of
the faraway stars against the blackness
opens as a visionary beacon
to guide our faraway dreams
of going there

Our planet's sister, Venus, is the queen
of the night sky – as a morning star, or
an evening star, she is the brightest
object in the heavens, save for the sun or moon
turning backwards, she doesn't
show us her dark side – though as the
goddess of love, she has one, of certainty

From my home in the desert
I watch Venus rise from over the mountains
a shimmering point of a certain expression
rising quickly, casting her diamonds of light
where the setting sun has just fallen, the
fiercely dense clouds in her atmosphere
hides her face from the earth

There may be life in the shimmering
density of those clouds, if so
I would not be at all surprised

Sometimes I Wonder Why

The setting sun has only minutes
until it crashes into the desert
behind the mountains
the stars are already
trying out their lights
in the wake of the sad, red
heavily descending sun

An eagle paints its shadow
on the cliff of the canyon wall
climbs into the mouth of
the falling sun, and
like God's feathered arrow
fades and falls

Here we stand, alone
on the mountain trail
under the two suns
hung in the red sky
one rising, one setting
each of us throwing two shadows
east and west
Without the vaguest idea, of
how this world works,
I sometimes wonder why
it turns at all, and what is holding
it in form, as it circles the faraway sun

Alone

Time still provides
a cunning memory
of the storms that
exhausted the ocean's energy

Paths from the sea
rise to the cliff wall
into the isolated cave
where the wood smoke still lingers

Alien drums pull
the forces of nature
into one beginning, perfectly
timed to the movement, of
the stars drawing their lights
in the dark night sky

Streams of moonlight, and
sheets of cold, rain water
are laced intricately together, they
fall as diamonds
through the cave opening
The memory of how
we held each other
closely for warmth
as we lay on the cold stone floor
throughout the long, long nights
is still with me

Now time has become
a withered, faded flower
a broken bone, a whispered chant
growing in the darkness, alone

The Sound of Heaven

There's no magic like the earth awakening
after winter is over, the first flowers
of a cold spring morning
are crafting poetry out of someone's dreams

My warmest thoughts are the beginning
of the morning coming up into the trees
sometimes the air is filled with just our sounds
can you hear it when it's rising

Movement can be as cold as ice
in your mood change, to define
the sweet taste of treason, as
it becomes the adjusted crime

You also said, the sound of heaven
must be made by two people

And I believed you

The Blue Tunnel into Tomorrow

The drums began when dusk fell
with the sun dying, painting
vermillion across the peaks
of the looming mountains, and
cold rain began falling

Four drums throbbing as heart beats
in unison, throughout the night

He lay before the fire
his breathing labored
eyes without sight

At daylight the rain turned to snow
then quickly back to rain, and
dark skies again

When the sun came through
the clouds later in the day
he gasped and shuddered once

As his spirit went through
the blue tunnel, into tomorrow

Then the drums were silent

Jesse Dances in L.A.

Jesse has a private honky-tonk, from
his single room in a fall-down, four
story brownstone, walkup on 6th Street
there he's known as a class act, among the hundreds
of vacant hustlers, lost on skid row

Jesse is both a bartender and his only client, and
he's easily served, because Jesse takes his bourbon
straight from the bottle, and when he gets right
he dances all by himself – although sometimes
he can sense her presence, there close beside him

When he sleeps, if the whiskey will let him go
he dreams once again of wire-walking
high above a canyon in a wind storm, among
howling black clouds, but the storm can't take him down
because Jesse's already fallen from heaven

Every morning he takes his place on the corner
down by the flower-market, he
dances on the sidewalk, to the sweet sounds
of, Melissa Manchester on his boom-box
he holds a sign: Help Jesse Dance
he's known to all as Dancing Jesse

Jesse, she'd said to him that evening
when she finally left him, can't you change for me
but Jesse doesn't know how, his soul is owned
by that amber liquid in the bottle
in a one room cell, down on 6th Street, and
late at night he flirts on that wire
high up in the sky – he can't fall, but
desperately wants to

I Dream of Flying

When I dream of flying
I'm part of the greater reach
into the clouds, floating wet and white
the force of summer in my hair
my hands shredding the clouds
moving as wings

Striking out across the open ocean
I rise and fall with the currents of the air
crest the waves that pull me downward
into the salty-spray, then
rise back into the clouds, finally
at last, I am truly alive

Tonight, when the moon rises above
the live oak trees in my yard
I will sight along the three leading stars
and I'll fly, the
gravity of the combined suns
in this star system
guiding me homeward

to Orion, far from the pulling earth
Then I'll awaken

Why Have You Then

Have you ever held a cold stone
in the fissured crook of your hand
until the warmth of your life
changed the balance of love and need
into blood in flesh on stone

Sometimes your feelings
are fickle like the wind
you don't change your mind
you just seem to change directions, the
way the wind bends the limbs of the trees
first one way, then the other

The thoughts behind your smile
are in another dimension
the cold energy from your touch
imprints me with wonder and
stays with me for days – the question remains:

Where are we now
it was always so simple before

The Trees Come Down at Night

What is it in the pine's
that moans and chills the night
is it the ghost, that
walk these old hills
late in the summer
when they know
the world is finally dying

The clouds hung low
over the mountains this morning
the rain slowly falls in rich drops
from the saddened sky

The trees walk up the mountain
into the clouds, and stay there
until the sun shines again
then creep back down in the night

The Lives of Sacred Trees

Alone and fearful, I follow the trail down to the creek
winding through the roots of ancient oaks, here
the water boils out from the depths of the earth
clarifies itself through polished stones, and
sand, made in another age by creeping, pushing ice

The shadows along the trail
are solemn, deep along the fern hill
a species of unknown birds sing – hidden in the depths
of the highest canopy of branches
they watch with their tiny eyes
the movement that human intrusion brings

I lay in the solitude of the forest
to absorb the odors of living leaves and grass
to taste and feel the damp odor of the soil
which is ever-wet from the rains that fall
with structured cadence and lie in the hollow
each drop of water is a pool of itself

When peace comes to me, I hear them then
the grumble of the oaks, their bodies held securely
in the black depths of living soil, by twisting roots
their masses of leaves building oxygen in the air
for other lives, they shelter and support

I have learned the language that they sing
their fissured boughs heavy with age
swinging with the rhythm
the deep bass of the live oaks
their branches touching the ground
the pines, their scarred bodies sway and sing
willows along the creek

bow down to the water and hum
in cadence with the taller trees around them

Then, I too join the chorus
my high-pitched voice, only heard internally, forms
a single note – but I am part of this secret earth
formed in religious solitude, found deep within
the bodies in this alien forest

I sing and sing until the trees shout me out
moving me farther away, down another dark
trail for unknown reasons, and now

I have now begun to fear the motives of the trees

April Is Her Name

April is her name, mother of our earth
she came back to her home in a scented storm
all of the birds in the universe
flying with her, singing to the sweetness of her form

In the earthly castle she waits in her rooms
alive with color, with defined dimensions
the lights from the windows look out over the sea
where the spirit of the afterlife
swam in with the tides to greet her

She sits in a painted window
in her shadow-darkened room
until the rising moon comes through the glass
covering her wet face, with pale-gold light

Flowers bloom in the air
from the breath she exhales
her beauty is without description, for
she is the first woman of this earth
millions of her followers, her sisters
chanting in unison: April, April, April, and
those of us that have known her
hide our faces
in shameful sight
afraid of both the darkness and the light

April, did you come back here just for me
alone and crippled in the night?

The Sound That Colors Make

The winter sun turns slowly westward
settling over the mountains, the clouds
painted from its falling, the collective sound of
their color is red

Night falls over the desert
as the sun dies, the saguaros cactus stand as giants
against the failing light
the sound of the night is black

Snow fell in the early morning
the mountains, now covered in new, wet snow
the rising sun promises a day of renewal
the sound of the snow is white

After a night of high wind
the morning breaks as the world turns
to meet the warmth of the rising sun
the sound of the clear sky is blue

The moon, when full, rises above
the Catalina mountains, first
there is only a glow of light, minutes
later the huge moon dominates
the black sky as it swiftly ascends upward
the sound of the rising moon is golden

After the winter rains, spring
comes to the desert, poppies
and the cactus blooms red and yellow, and
the sound of the newly emerging grass is green

One can touch the stars
as they begin to emerge, from
the black-on-black heavens in faraway space
the sound the stars make as they sparkle in the night
are the glitter of carelessly thrown diamonds
burning from an internal fire

When autumn comes to the mountains
the grass becomes dormant
losing its color, many
of the trees are dropping
their leaves onto the earth and
into the wind
the sound of their color becomes brown

Dark clouds built up over the mountains
the temperature fell, and the sun went away
as the rain began falling
the wind and rain so cold, and
the sound of the sky became gray again

Lost Like Me

I still think of you late at night
when the globe of the warm earth
is in eternal darkness
when God's own light
has gone into another world
then I remember you in your tilted youth
tasting the colors of the skies
in those stained years
when you were lost like me

The pulse of your heartbeat
measured by your breast beneath my hand
your driving blood beating against mine
the vast distance from your eyes
to mine

My need for you
drawing me closer
to the words that are coming
from the sweetness of your April smile
paying me deeply for my troubles

sometimes forgetting that you too were
lost like me

I Sing as the Ocean

My tracks over yours
in wet sand, on lonely beaches
lost in the mist at the end of sight
the sea oats bent in the ocean wind
the tide ever alive, ever changing
goes up the beach and back again

Can you touch me
from the safety of your distance?
can you see me lost out here alone
depending solely upon
the pull of the gulf-stream
for my life

Wind-crumpled clouds
hung in a trembling rhythm
in the deep blue of empty space
between me and the sea
when they find us, will we be together, and

will you ever hear me sing as the ocean again?

She Dances in the Trees

He brought her down the lane
through the orchard, in a wheelchair
the trees blooming pink and white, the wind scattering
the fallen petals into the air, she smiled
remembering

Her hair was gray now, her shoulders bent
in age, the sickness that had overtaken
her body – refusing all attempts to arrest it

He left her there alone, as she had asked
she sat and thought, and wondered

She felt the music of Sibelius
playing in her mind
standing without assistance
she began to dance

As she danced the years fell away from her
her hair darkened – the wrinkles disappeared
her beauty bloomed as the trees
in her mind
She swirled to the sound of the violins
dancing through the apple trees in spring bloom
a young girl now – and in love once again

They found her there, lying in the spring grass
a smile etched into the beauty of her face
apple blossoms drifting about her

The magical sound of Sibelius remained in the trees

It Was in the Summer

The trail began near her home
it went upward toward the hill
to the abandoned house
that slumped there, under
many generations of the summer sky
where only spirits lived

Trellised grapes were ripening on rusted wires
a weathered, long-neglected jasmine
at the corner of the fallen porch
permeated the air with the scent of mystery
it had never failed to bloom, generation by generation
though no human life had influenced it

We sat upon the grass under the oak tree
still damp from the dew of the night
twenty years separated our individual lives
my life greatly complicated by obligations
her life, young and pure
complicated only by innocence
then she told me that she was in love with me

My resolve died by the second, as
I tasted the unavoidable sin when I kissed her

My Hometown

For most of my life
the broad expanse of America
has been my hometown
I've lived it – lived within it, the
dark land we call freedom, that
my ancestors fought and died for
From shore to shore
border to border
I have yet to meet
a town that I walked into alone
that didn't joyfully take me in
as a returning, prodigal son
Cheap motels, dingy restaurants, and
tired women have sheltered me, from
myself – from the cold, the rain, and
from that big ball of fire up in the sky
that continues to burn the painted earth
I have sung, danced, and wept
with outcast like myself, and
with people that supposedly knew better
I have known love with only a smile
to proclaim it, still voiceless inside me
America, will you be there to comfort me
when my friends are all gone
when my country has finally died, and
the remaining nameless, faceless children have
discovered what they've lost
at the end of each pitted, nameless road
with no beginning, with no ending

Alvarado Street

With you in MacArthur Park, on Sunday afternoon
underneath the tall eucalyptus trees
on a park-bench – the sun warm, sparkling
in the waters of the lake, the
small boats passing in circles
through the shadows, then back into the
sunlight again – I kiss you softly, feel the
pulse of your heart in my hand

I'm holding your small, warm hand
when we walked down Alvarado Street
your love for me in the smile that was only mine
I experience the love for you all over again
as I remember these sacred moments
when we were young and didn't yet know
how fleetingly cold, life can become

Your soft hand touches my face, when you
kiss me in my sleep, and
whisper that yesterday can come back
to us, – that we can be together again
in another life, another dimension
if we will it to be, in our individual dreams

Maybe, but let's try anyway

Let There Be Light

Where in dim rooms, poverty shown exacting
there exists the smallest light, creating
the potential for shadows to bloom

A small house at the end of a dirt road, overgrown
with weeds, is forsaken, lonely – empty
of all life, or anything human

A thin point of light from a crescent moon
entered the dusty windows, a piano began softly
playing, *The Moonlight Sonata*

The melody of the sonata blends with the dim light
filtering through the windows
the small house becomes
a symphony of light and sound

Two shadows emerged from the darkness, and
began slow-dancing against the stained wallpaper
of flowers on the opposite wall

When the music ended, he bowed and kissed her
then a passing cloud blocked the moonlight, and
the shadows went away together, back into the dark, then

silence fell like a shroud after the close of the music

Off Biloxi – An Uncertain Day

Sails stand out at the curve
of the 20-fathom line
bent to the ocean winds

Out here, the ocean, is
one shade bluer than the sky

The wind in your hair
the wind carrying your laughter away
your eyes clouded with doubt

You're the only thing on my mind
out here in the sun

I keep following you
out into the ocean
further and further away
from the certain security
of the shore

The white-capped waves, now
coming over the side
of the leaning boat
your laughter, more subdued

My concern has begun to unfold
over unnamed storms
that we'd likely brought out here with us

And the sky beginning to darken

July

Your small, round breasts
are silken to my touch

The trees along the ridge
are shedding leaves
in the height of summer

The leaves writhe and wither
in this rainless season of drought

July, will you walk slowly
away from me
so that losing sight of you
overcomes me softly?

Leaving the fragrance
of your body

Suspended in the air for hours

Return from Nowhere

He came back the same way
that he'd left the first time, by train
in another age – another dimension
when his hair was still brown, and
his eyes were the color of the sky
of a spring morning

He dropped off the train at the crossing
of the train yard – a mile from the depot
the building much older now
but still brown, chipped, peeling
in the same place as 65 years ago, when he'd
boarded – to ride away into another life
far from the poverty he'd known – that he'd lived

He walked down the tracks toward River Avenue
the neighborhood curiously intact, but
all black lives now in the old crooked houses
poverty trading across generations
from white to black, but still
poor, run down, and sad

He crossed over the trestle, not quite so high
as when he was a boy – the brown river
swirling around the pilings, the odor of creosote
rising on the damp, summer air

After standing and looking at the old house
where he'd been born, for a long, long time
he rationalized: let someone else carry this burden
that's been mine much too long, then
he walked back to the depot, to wait for the train

He walked straighter, leaving the burden lying in the street

Loraine

Loraine sat in front of the open window
the night breeze soundlessly moved the curtains
she had been crying and thinking for hours
damn your soul she said aloud, then drew the cross
from her forehead to her stomach
then, shoulder to shoulder, touching her mouth
I didn't mean that, she murmured

She corrected herself and re-crossed
taking away the apology, yes
damn it, I did mean it, damn your soul to hell
she cursed the man who had betrayed her
Loraine was waiting for the light of the moon
before venturing out into the night
to consummate her resolution

The full moon rose immense and golden
through the trees, throwing long shadows
through the darkness, down to the water's edge
she stepped through the French doors
onto the lawn, the grass damp, – cold to her bare feet
the tears had dried upon her face
her eyes narrowed in hard commitment

She dropped her robe onto the pier
standing naked in the moonlight
she removed the ring from her finger
and with another curse threw it into the lake
it fell without a sound, without a splash, and
never would it disgrace another hand
the way that it had disgraced her life

Laughing now she dove from the pier
into the night-chilled waters of the lake
moonlight moving across the waters
to guide her long swim across the lake
and back again – she emerged from the water
wrung the water from her long, dark hair
the cold water had washed all semblance
of her former life – she had emerged a new person
she was now free from him, forever

It had begun to softly rain
as she was putting on the robe
the moon had retreated behind the thin clouds
a pale glow illuminated the trees, water
glistening on the new spring-leaves
She placed her hands on her swollen stomach
when she felt the baby moving inside her
your name is Rain, she said to the new life
that shared her body
boy or girl it doesn't matter
it's just the two of us now Rain
the name had come to her out of the clouds

Loraine was smiling as she walked
back to the darkened house, when
she felt the baby kick, there's Rain, she said

An Imperfect Expectation

The clouds where you live
are fragile white
pure as a virgin's kiss
on her sacred wedding night

The sky is descending
to bring warm rain, to the
pastures and trees
in the green light

But the clouds where I live
are terrible dark – toiling away there
high above the earth tonight
in the storm of lightning and wind
a voice of deep frustration
for there's not a virgin in sight

What Is a Heart

She awakened as the dawn light
crept inside the small room
through the panes of glass in the window
reflecting off the mirror – then into my eyes

I lay naked on my side, in the bed
where we had made love, throughout
the long, starless night

then

we both laughed
at the absurdity of sin being a component
of the poverty within us

She said to me, I shall leave now, and
I shall take something personal of
yours with me

Saying this, she smiled her death mask, and
reaching inside my chest she removed
that object that pushes life through my body
Why not – I'll not need that where I'm going
I said this in a loud, defiant voice
the dust motes shining in the new light
turning away from the noise
huddled in one corner of the room
She nodded her agreement – leaving through the
open window – her body, thin as smoke and mist
rising in the early morning sky, then
the clouds enveloped her

I went back to sleep, having exhausted
the thoughts of her that had gone into my head
after dying in my eyes

The Sun Can Rise So Quickly

Over a lonely hill
and start a new day
of making shadows
the crickets can sing
in the grass alongside the creek
the grapes have finally dried
on the aged, twisted vines
the butterflies have gone away
to some other place
where it's still warm, and
flowers are blooming

it's going to be a long time
from now, but summer
is sure to come back here
for those of us
that so desperately need it

more now in the later years
than before

I Still Think of You Late at Night

When the globe of the warm earth
is in eternal darkness
when God's own light
has gone into another dimension
then I remember you in your tilted youth
tasting the colors of the skies
in those stained years
when you were lost like me

I haven't been back to the earth
in a long time – is it still a cold, lonely place?
without a defined beginning or ending
from the depth of your eyes
to the vault of the endless days
that dare the rise of the moon

Will you walk slowly away from me?
so that losing sight of you
comes to me slowly

The Spring Rain

Falls silently through
the newly leafed branches of the trees
the days of warm sunshine, and
the new silken grass, humming birds, and butterflies
have come back here again

I tried not to think of someone
that I knew a long time ago, but
she is forever here
her mouth soft and sweet
like the odor of this wet May morning
her eyes, deep pools of questions
about things, for which there are no answers

After the rain, afternoon shadows lie very deep
on the grass, under the living
canopy of trees, reaching into the May skies
the sun returning to me again, and
believe me, though I'm far away
the memory of you lives within me

always and forever

A Rainbow Fell

From a cold, dark, cloudless sky
a sky that was totally without rain
streaming colors against the velvet blackness
before crashing into the earth
of the winter desert

At the point where the rainbow fell
stood a woman, shrouded
by swirling, green mist
that rose from the ground
around her feet

She beckoned to me, with
a hand that glowed from
an internal fire, and though she
didn't speak verbally
her message was personal
to me, I listened with bated breath

The silent language that she spoke
was ancient Latin
when she smiled
a halo of blue light surrounded her face
I stepped back in awe
her beauty was not of this world
and would never be – she said this to me:

Diu te quaesivi – in hoc universo et aliis, nunc mecum redi, omnia dimittuntur

The Light Slowly Moves Across

The arc of a troubled sky
describing a rainbow
in three timid colors
a noble ending to the rain
still threatening with thunder
behind the mountains

A sunken tree in the river
lifts one leafless branch
to the sky, still grasping in vain
for the sun, even in death
it's moving slowly
swaying like it once did when alive
moving in the strumming
rhythm of the current
of the living, growing river

Afternoon shadows are dark
on the grass, under the living
canopy of trees, reaching into the June skies
believe me, though I'm far away
the memory of you lives within me
part of the silence, in the shadows

underneath the trees

Do You Remember the Summer?

Down by the river, the dragon flies
dipping down to kiss the water
the willow limbs dragging, into
the swift current of the river
the trees on the hill
a dark green wall of wonder

Why didn't the birds sing
the day the clouds accumulated
in one corner of the sky
just over the place
where I waited alone for you

A cold day in the summer
more than a lifetime ago, now
the sound of my life is only
one gray note, on a summer dying

The Bruha Katrina

She was born off Africa
rising from the dark ocean with malice
in her non-human heart, spinning
dark wind and vast volumes of water
from the center of her satanic being
the white rain continued to fall
heavily from the fell-sky
the integrity of the near world
chased across thousands of miles
of dark salt-sea

Possessed of a singular, damaged soul
the wind-song of the dense, clouds
spun around the center of her vortex
that portends certain destruction
when land is broached

He walked out onto to the beach
supported against the wind
by a heavy stick in each hand
naked, pale in the darkness of the storm
he looked upward to the sky in defiance, shouting
why did you let her come here, with this destruction?

I have followed the instructions
Of the Sermon on The Mount
I have been loyal to a fault
Ten-foot waves washed over the islands
out to the west, in the Gulf
the old man felt this happening
he could feel the drowning of the low sand-dunes
only minutes later a sea wall of water
20 feet high, took him off his feet

riding atop the monstrous storm surge
as it drove miles inward, tearing apart the land
crushing everything in its path

He continued shouting to the mystery in the sky
about the meek inheriting the earth
is that too a lie, if it's not – when will it happen
some of us are still believers

Three days later, when the water had begun
to recede – they found him high in the branches
of an ancient live oak that had withstood the fury
of the terrible wind and water, his pale, naked body
was largely untouched
An old woman helped remove his body from the tree
she coughed; I suppose that he's now inherited the earth
that's what he always believed in, that's what he often
preached – the meek shall inherit the earth

She looked upwards in wonder, when
she heard the sound of a low-laughter
coming from the pure white clouds above her
caught and suspended in the deep blue sky

No Cold Stone Can Hide Her

No damp earth can contain her
she now walks through oceans
of undulating grass
under the warm brown suns
in another dimension
spinning the hope of eternal spring
stacked clouds of living voices
into the hands of God almighty
swarms of suns in his hooded eyes
reborn into the greater universe
perpetually creating cycles
of compassion, love and trust
for those that love her now
and generations of unborn children
that will celebrate her living and dying
to give back life, love, forgiveness, forever and ever

I know that she's coming back here again
she told me so – I believe everything
that she's ever said

Lost in America

She found me lost in America
a child of the war-damaged generation
she was an uncertain woman
lost like me

I wrote her story into a poem, but
she found my insincere
approach to living was without merit, and
she moved away from me

On a cold night in January
when my life was upside-down
the moon inverted, the river
that I lived in ran backwards
she walked out of my poem

My life as I previously knew it
became vacant – one line at a time
I had to find someone that knew my verse, and
wasn't afraid of where the poems
took them, at that point
Mystery walked into my life

Two Generations in the Repose of Sleep

Two generations from where they died
I walked across their graves and cried

In the weeded lot, where
our house would have been
was a stone, their names
carved across the granite
born this date – died this date
two of them together lay

Someone above was asking
do they rest in peace, and
will they eventually come back
here to the living world?

I answered for them
when we celebrate life
death will inevitably follow

No one knows where or when
the beginning
or the ending will be, except
that it will surely be there

just wait until you see it coming

Writing in the Night

A thin, pale, angle of light

From a swiftly descending crescent

Of moon, came through his window, and

Began writing, unaided

The many tokens of his faults

Line by line

Until the grey-planked, paint-peeled wall

Was filled with written condemnation

His sad, old, tired eyes

Released the emotion, of

Many years of never having cried

Until the freedom of finally telling the truth

Escaped him, and

It set him free

Morning Rain

I ran in the rain this morning, before daylight

Just a gentle mist, a soft weeping

That wet my hair slowly

I kept looking for you

Behind every tree and park bench

I suppose that you're as close as the telephone

As far away as several hours

I know the rain makes me lonely

Even though it's so soft, that

I can't hear it falling

A Cold Slice of the Moon

Hangs inverted, connected to the earth

By thin webs of force

Against the black of January's night

Against the black of the foreboding sky

Light years from the city

Connected by the cold air of January

In these lonely hills

Black on black, and

So unforgiving cold

On the Ridge Road to Summerland

The sunrise warms up the morning

In a ritual that is more than the earth

Beginning a new day

Shadows are falling

From the crosses of martin gourds

Hung, stark against the rising sun

Still, I move one memory from you

Until my most important memory

Becomes singularly my own again

Close to our Summerland home

On old Ridge Road
That will never go away

Your Laughter Hung in the Air

In the space where we sat

Before moving quickly up the hill

Fortunately, your smile

Stayed in its customary place

But your eyes ask me questions

That I can't answer

When Tommy Died

Is it the wind

In the pines that moan

Is it the ghost

That walk these old hills

Late in the summer

When they know the world is dying

In a small pond, surrounded by pine trees

The cicadas are singing the death knell of my friend

When the muddy water gave him back

To those of us who waited in terror

For his return

Throughout my life

When I hear the sound of the singing pines

The ghostly song of the cicadas
In my mind, I go back

To that lonely place, where and when

Tommy died – on a Saturday of certain sorrow

A Storm Is Coming

Uncontrolled motion of clouds

Loose in the autumn skies

The trees bent from the constant

Force of the sky

The air becoming progressively colder

It isn't quite winter yet

But I can feel it

There's another season of

Storms coming

The Thoughts Behind Your Smile

The thoughts behind your smile

Are in another dimension

The energy from your touch

Stays with me for days

You had to hold your arms

Out to me, remember

Because I get so cold

Even in the summer

Is Music More Than Black Patches

On lines of paper, and

Will we ever learn to

Live again, after we go separately away
Is there something else that I haven't done

That one time felt so important

To you

In the dimly lit room, playing there

A piano, a saxophone – shadows

From the candles, the lost melody

Playing still – even when we went away

And the musical symbols
Walked away from the page

September Is a Brown Warm Song

The cloudless skies, the

Leaves on the trees, just beginning to turn

Butterflies brightly hung

In the space over the flowers

Birds drawing circles in the liquid air

Autumns almost here again

It's been gone a long time

But finally, it's coming back

Bringing the painted leaves

And soon afterwards, the acid touch of winter

I Often Think of Someone I Knew Long Ago

Her mouth was soft and sweet

Like the sweet odor

Of a wet spring morning

Her eyes were deep pools

Of questions about things

For which there are no answers

Can you pay me deeply

For my smallest insecurities

Once so important, now fading away

In the failing light

Remembering, it was so long ago
That I'd largely forgotten to say

That I still love you

The Rising Sun Brought a Textured Morning

Light filled the sky, the scent of rain filled the air

The singing of birds, rejoicing to have escaped the night

High above on the spiraling trail, she

Followed me, with the dark eyes of storm clouds

And there we were in a matrix of light, sound, and wind

Far from the summit of the mountain, afraid to go further

Not from the threat of the height, but from each other

He Held a Lotus Flower in His Hands

It was bitterly cold in the mountains, but
he wore only a saffron robe and sandals

We are very high up, aren't you cold,
I asked him

He smiled – his brown creased face
spoke to me, although he hadn't said a word

I don't live here – I'm from another place
where it is eternally summer

I came here for you, if you are ready for enlightenment
to help you find the way of the Zen

I followed him until we reached the summit
he held my hand in his

then together we stepped out into the sky

Somewhere a Woman Is Crying

I awoke in the dead of night

From a deep sleep

When the ormolu clock struck twelve

Softly chiming

I heard a woman crying

Somewhere in the house

Though I live alone

In trepidation I searched every room

Finding nothing

Until I returned to bed, then I heard her again

She's not in the rooms of this old, creaking house

She's inside my head

Where she's been these many years, and

I am never really alone

Time

One flower drawn on yellow paper

One thought turned to moving

In a living rhyme

Moving slowly, with delicate purpose

Over the green earth, the blue ocean, and

The blue sky above you

Writing with my finger

Over your naked spine

Time, Time, Time

I Wonder Where

I awakened in the night

Not sensing your presence

Wondering where you'd gone

I thought, one talon

I'm one talon deep

In a world of electrical friction

Not unfeeling, not falling, just

The fear of finding the claw

Of waiting, a stranger lost

In a foreign land

Far from recovery

If I'm ever needed, again

In the real world

Of where you're living

Underneath the Whispers

We lay as one, underneath the whispers

After making love, and

Began counting the stars, hung

In the dark emptiness – the home

Of the great unknown that has never

Heard a prayer, although they've

Been shouted skyward by humans

Throughout eternity

The Ruined South

In the year 1865, three young men, two of them brothers, the other a first cousin, had been fighting in the defense of Atlanta. They rationalized that the cause they once believed in was an illusion – totally without merit. They left the battlefield and began the journey home. They became deserters – renegades. Home is where the heart is ... isn't that what they say? Except, in these times, home was only in the heart. The South was largely destroyed. Few homes were left standing.

One

The sun had dropped low over the opposite hills, painting the low clouds behind them, blood red.

Whippoorwills called again, and the evening became quiet as death.

She shuddered as she felt the chill come over her.

The premonition – the cold realization of her own vulnerability ran through her blood. She felt the presence of her lost husband – gone to war

She knew that life is uncompromisingly certain: birth, trial, death; coming in a straight, unwavering line of light

Then the final darkness of the eternal night

Two

It was a long time before the lieutenant slept
he was visited by the ghost of his memories, and he
dealt with them as best he could

About midnight the clear night sky became obscured by clouds
both the quarter moon and stars disappeared, and
a fine mist of rain began to fall onto last year's dried leaves

He hunkered down, covered by his slicker, listening
to the clicking of the small water onto the leaves
he was carried back to a gentler time before the war

She swept across the sanded floor in her new dress
her dark hair shining in the light of the lanterns
she smiled for him, lighting up the room

He took her home that night – they sat in the buggy
out in the road – the lathered horse shaking his bridle to continue

She confessed to him that she loved him, that
she would marry him, and before he had to leave
would he just come back to her, she pleaded

The rain continued throughout the night
becoming harder after daylight
She had returned to him time and again as he fitfully slept
each time she brought an old memory of their last days
together – brilliant in its reality, but bitter
for him to swallow in his dry throat

He awakened with the vision of her naked body
her long, dark hair on the pillow
the scent of her body, strongly in his mind

Three

They had fought a skirmish earlier in the day
he had taken a slight shrapnel wound

He lay on his back against the hard earth
staring at the deep blackness of space

The moon described a crescent, pale against the dense cluster
of stars in the milky way

A track of burning light streaked across the vault of the black sky, and
disappeared into the near curve of the horizon

Dew had fallen – wetting his hand that lay in the grass beyond his head
he moved his hand, and tasted the wetness from the sky

His eyes moved to the sparkling stars above him – his thoughts wafted away
lost in the greater expanse of the hostile heavens, but the pain brought him
back
He thought of his wife in Mississippi – more than a year now since her last
letter
is she thinking of me tonight, he wondered, in his solitude

The blood-crusted on his shoulder had begun to weep again
he tried to adjust the bandage … it was wet

The cannon fire had not abated since early afternoon
the heavy guns of the United States Army continued to fire against
the lightly fortified, ill-equipped troops that held the high ground

An owl uttered his lonesome call – somewhere over the river
another owl answered him – loud in the stillness between the
cannon fire

I hear you, he whispered – *I don't know what you're saying, but I plainly hear*
you speaking to me

Four

He sat under the pines at the top of the hill
watching the ending of the day
he heard the bone-saw working in the tent nearby
a young boy crying out, for his lost arm

Thin dark clouds lay horizontally across the path
of the sad, red, descending battle-sun
the sky turning pink, then progressively
shifted through various shades of red
finally disappearing entirely

In its wake, a single star suddenly flared
shimmering in the after-glow in the wake
of the pale, fading-light

His cousin walked over and sat beside him
they wordlessly passed a bottle of whiskey, that
he'd taken from the hospital tent

The magic of the evening was too pronounced
to be broken by words

There was a holiness about the evening
that defied description, both of them relieved
individually
…for

pieces of their lives had passed before them
that bloody day, bloomed and died in the final sun

An orderly approached them – he saluted
James Overstreet has died, Sir – you said to let you know
they looked at each other – their eyes downcast
he was from the hollow down the road from them
back home in Mississippi – they drank to him and wept

They left the battlefield that night, the three of them

Five

Lightning flashed, connecting to the ground in long, brilliant streaks of fire

The air was heavy with the soul of the fast-approaching storm

Spirits of long-dead soldiers turned in the damp ground
from the vibrations of the thunder
reverberating cannon like
through the stratified layers of Southern clay and sand

The cool breeze coming down the valley, became a gust, and
the gust became a gale, as horizontal sheets of cold rain
engulfed the riders

He reached out before him, touching the hand extended to him
through the curtain of white rain

Lightning extended from hand to hand, coursed
through his arm, across his body
His beard glowed from the fire of the other world
and
the companion riders fell back from him
afraid of what they'd seen

Six

The old officer watched the men disappear down the trail
until they could no longer be seen – though the jangling harness of the horses
could still be heard

The stub of his arm throbbed – hot bolts of pain ran through the damaged nerve
cells, tendons, and shattered bone

He extended the screaming arm before him
and
from it beheld a vision of five thousand bedraggled men
many without guns, charging
a fortified redoubt of twelve-pound cannons

Dense smoke covered the hillside, concealing the location
of the awful din

The awesome force of the Rebel Yell, coming from five thousand
throats – carried him directly into the mouth of hell

From the ground, where he'd been thrown, he looked upward
beyond the smoke into the heart of God's tortured sky above him

The remainder of his arm spewed a fountain of crimson
framed dark against the blue, of eternal heaven

They had skirted the battle that had ensued
riding around it – from the sound they knew it was terrible

They found the captain on the road
he had bled to death

Seven

Light filtering through the pines, falls on the new earth
piled precariously on the pine-straw littered hill

Money, fame, fortune; nothing matters when the white worms
are at the last remaining flesh

The cold earth, the damp, everlasting ground, is the only safe haven
now for the carpetbagger, mean and dead
dead
in the warm night and eternal darkness

No light can penetrate the mound of red clay, that
holds the decaying bones, fast, in its eternal embrace

The earth trembles when the thunder of summer storms
fall over the Alabama hills

Bones rattle in the ground, and
the wind sighs in the tall pines that
overlook the unmarked grave
Carpetbagger, why did you come down here ... only for your death

Eight

Long shadows from the towering pines
lay cool on the road of Sweet Alabama
in the near summer – rift with hostility

The blood hadn't dried on the red-clay roads, but
already the Southern birds fall fleetingly to the rough
sap, scarred limbs, from musket balls made

There they hang, as black triangles
swinging into the certain
fall of dusk – after the firing had ended

Will you recover from this – they ask mockingly, in unison
to the three bodies lying in the road
as they swooped lower

The uniforms they wore had originally been blue
their boots and weapons had been taken

Nine

It had been cloudy early in the evening

As the night progressed the clouds were blown away by a pervasive, northern
wind

The black-night sky was clear, save for the myriad of twinkling stars
in dense complications of geometric confusion
spun across the vault of the unholy heavens

Occasionally, dying remnants of other worlds burned fiery streaks
across the black sky

The night was quiet and calm in the darkness of the ruined countryside
wrought in blood and destruction from the lost … never-forgiven war

Unable to sleep, he thought about the terrible things
that he'd witnessed – participated in
it saddened him – he asked himself, what was it for

Ten

Dusk dark began to settle down over the lonely woods
the sun dipped below the horizon, and
only a feeble light remained

The woods behind him were completely dark now
bull-bats dived low over the road – insects hummed
in the trees, and the wind that had blown high throughout the day
finally lay down – there was no gunfire
it had become deathly quiet

The first star appeared in the pink space where the sun had fallen
then
God walked out onto the pale clouds … the pink sky
shuddered and bent, under the awesome weight of the creator

He heard the sound of approaching horses, and
sought shelter behind the stacked logs
he could hear their low voices, as they looked for the trail
in the gloaming
Was it them or us – he was afraid of the heavy beating of his heart
would give him away … then he heard the familiar accent
of his home, and audibly sighed in relief

Eleven

Night fell – clouds drifted over the face of the three-quarter moon – casting
shadows over the red-clay road.

They passed fewer farms as they got further away from Selma
people living near the road came out of their houses when they were awakened
by a dog's barking.

They watched the shapes of dim riders, approaching, then passing silently as
ghostly shapes in the dark.

They heard the jangle of bridles and the sound of moving leather
the soft clop of the horse's hooves in the dirt road, then silence.

They stood there for several minutes after they passed, speculating if the riders
were friend or foe – or even living occupants of this earth.

The riders themselves asked the question: were, these people friend or foe
They were now, only a four-days ride from home
what was left there, they wondered … anything

Twelve

Riding throughout the night they came to the bank, of
the Tombigbee River soon after daylight
fog lay heavy over the water, the
river high – from heavy rain upstream
Cypress and tulip trees stood ghostly out into the river
there was no ferry for many miles in either direction
swimming the horses across was the only option

He rode down the muddy bank, his
horse fighting the bridle, the pack horse balking
he lost the rope from the pack horse behind him
his brother caught the rope in the water, and
swam the river with all three horses
they drifted a hundred yards downstream in the current
clambered up the far bank, into the woods
on the far side

Four cabins burned to the ground
on the red-clay road above the river
thin smoke rose from the ashes
four families of poor whites
sat on the bluff above the road
across from where their houses had stood
three of the younger men
digging a grave nearby
there's calvary up ahead, they said
burned us out last night
the men rode on

A mile up the road two more cabins
lay smoldering in the heat of the
sorrowful morning
several blacks poked around in the ashes

searching for anything salvageable
one squinted against the sun
they burned us out, Captain
thought we were white, I reckon
there's eight of them

They found them less than a
mile away – cooking breakfast
four were shot as they sat on the ground
the horses broke their tether's
running down the road

The four men remaining scattered into the trees
the blacks were there in a few minutes
they carried away all that was valuable
the four bodies they left
for the turkey vultures, already
circling high overhead

Thirteen

They went into a farm yard to water their horses
a single woman with four children, shoeless, dressed in rags
came off the porch to watch them

There were no animals there in the yard
not a pig, a chicken, or a guinea, not even a dog

She refused to take the money they offered
so, they left it on top of the stone well
the children, in a virtual trance of hunger, said nothing

They rode from the poverty-racked yard of dried mud
without saying another word – angry at the causation

At the road they stopped the horses, looking back
the five of them stood there at the well as before
none of them moving

The lieutenant rode back to the well, and
handed the frail woman four, five-dollar gold pieces
they were donated by the very-dead
carpetbagger, they had left in the woods
she took them – kissed his hand

She said to him, a letter came last week
he died in Atlanta – they said he was a hero
tears ran in two parallel lines down her face
despite this, she smiled, remembering him

The cross of gourds swayed in the listless morning wind
up ahead the day's first dust-devil spun up the road
shaking the leaves of the cottonwood trees

Heat waves had begun rising above the old fields
gone to weeds and waste

He felt a chill go down his spine
remembering something awful that he couldn't
completely identify, asking himself – why did this have to happen?

He was now only a day's ride from home – and he was very afraid
of something that he couldn't define

Fourteen

He rode through the night, anxious to get home

The wind in the Southern pines is the breath of the Lord of the World.
sometimes his ways are hostile – not always understood by those capable of it

Never mind the simpler ones who were born to suffer for unknown reasons
he stared around him at the black mass of trees, moving in the wind
as he turned off the road

The crescent moonwalked over the tops of the swaying limbs – and her spirit
image came to him glowing from its pale light

He rode up to the cabin right after the sun came up
there was no sign of life

The cabin was intact, as he had left it … she wasn't there

He found her grave, underneath the red oak tree, he
had built a swing for her, hung it from the tree's lowest limb

He sat in it now, looking around the yard … the flowers she'd
planted were blooming – the bluebird box had chicks in it – he could hear them

He said very quietly: *I'm home now* – but home is not the same, with her not
in it.

Fifteen

An hour before daylight he awakened from a troubled dream, but couldn't
remember what it was about

He had slept in the barn – on the scant amount of hay that was there

Finding the courage, he went inside the cabin and spread the thin feather
mattress out on the bed.

He lay there in the darkness, feeling the presence of his dead wife's spirit in
the room with him.

The tattered curtains moved in the open windows – the floor softy creaked with
footsteps

The room suddenly became cold from the wind coming into the room from the
gray world beyond.

Just as quickly, he was comforted by her reaching out to him
the cold evaporated, and he was touched by a sensation of warmth, as the
breeze changed.
Then he slept, no longer threatened by the spirit world
although, he couldn't explain that either

Home … he thought, what does that mean anymore